Velvet Waters

Canyon Walls

Looking toward Rock Creek Canyon in Dungeon Canyon

Velvet Waters
Canyon Walls

A Lake Powell Adventure
By Colin Warren

Northland Press Flagstaff, Arizona

CONTENTS

The dawn of a new day

INTRODUCTION

For centuries, the Colorado River has served as both inspiration and challenge for those who have encountered its awesome splendor. The ceaseless flowing of its raging torrents through the sparsely populated mountain regions of Colorado, Utah, and Arizona eventually becomes a gentle trickle by the time the waters flow south into the Gulf of California. The river brought life to regions which otherwise were desert land, and the endless flow of water acts as a natural sculptor, carving towering cliffs with seemingly bottomless canyons from the mountains through which it passes.

Major John Wesley Powell, an early explorer of the river, wrote from Glen Canyon, Utah, in July 1869, saying: "One could almost imagine that the walls had been carved with a purpose, to represent giant architectural forms. In the deep recesses of the walls we find springs, with mosses and ferns on the moistened sandstone." He also told of the river " . . . sweeping around these bends, undermines the cliffs in places. Sometimes the rocks are overhanging; in other curves, curious narrow glens are found. Through these we climb by a rough stairway, perhaps several hundred feet, to where a spring bursts out from under an overhanging cliff, and where cottonwoods and willows stand, while along the curves of the brooklet oaks grow, and other rich vegetation is seen, in marked contrast to the general appearance of naked rock."

The land Powell described is now part of the Glen Canyon National Recreation Area which includes the magnificent Lake Powell, a lake created from the visions inspired by the mighty Colorado. The imposing terrain, recorded on the pages of this book, was actually the result of man viewing nature and deciding to change the course of the awesome Colorado.

It was 1922 when the Colorado River Compact was signed. Legislators in the Southwest decided to alter the flow of the mighty Colorado, changing its course so that it could bring water needed to enable cities within the region to grow. This meant creating a dam to serve as a storage facility so that the natural fluctuations of water volume could be controlled. That dam, now known as Glen Canyon Dam, was authorized on April 11, 1956, with construction started on October 15 of that same year.

When the Glen Canyon Dam was finally completed on September 15, 1963, man

1

had successfully altered one of nature's wonders, creating a new spectacle as awesome in its own way as the land which inspired Major Powell. The Colorado River was finally controlled, its waters forming Lake Powell. The river had been transformed into a serene waterway winding through some of the most magnificent and inaccessible regions of the United States.

The construction of the dam and the creation of Lake Powell were not accomplished without tremendous controversy. The Colorado River's natural flow sustained plant and animal life which could not be supported by the changes created by Lake Powell and the Glen Canyon Dam. For example, the river annually carried over 140 million tons of red sediment through Glen Canyon. Now, this sediment is trapped in the upper reaches of Lake Powell, a situation which is expected to cause the complete filling of the lake within 150 to 200 years and form a waterfall over Glen Canyon Dam.

The trapping of the sediment has meant the slow erosion of downstream beaches, whose sand was once replenished by the natural flow of the river. The fluctuating amount of water released through the dam does not allow an adequate release of sediment to prevent this measured destruction.

The surface level of Lake Powell fluctuates each spring when mountain snows thaw and cause the lake to rise. Gradually, over the summer months, some of this water is released and the surface level recedes. This has created perhaps the world's largest "bathtub ring," a white line readily visible against the red-orange cliffs. Such fluctuations also drown much of the vegetation in the area and leach nutrients from the soil.

There have been positive changes in the ecosystem of the area, particularly from the view of sportsmen. The introduction of the dam has altered the water temperature, which previously varied from forty degrees in winter to eighty-five degrees in summer. Now the water temperature remains constant below the dam, permitting new forms of fish life to be introduced. Trout can successfully breed in the river just below the dam and striped bass from Lake Mead swim up the river to spawn in the cold water.

The terrain once enjoyed by Major Powell has been flooded, eliminating prehistoric cliff dwellings and the natural art formed by the ceaseless flow of water. However, Lake Powell, with its nearly 2,000 miles of shoreline, has developed its own beauty, creating a new attraction for tourists. Thousands of boaters now explore its velvet waters. Five marinas are spread along the lake's 186-mile length, recreation facilities enjoyed by almost two million visitors each year. Yet few have been so stirred as Colin Warren, who decided to explore as much as possible of the grandeur of the land and the water so beautifully altered by man.

Warren, who worked at Lake Powell for several years, chose to make his trip accompanied only by his dog, Ely. They would travel in a seventeen-foot canoe fitted with outrigger pontoons, a small sail, and a watertight compartment. The trip would be a leisurely one, a fact that led him to name the boat *Homba Goshli,* a Zulu phrase meaning "to go slow gently."

The trip, expected to take a year, was carefully planned. Three month supplies of food, including dog food, medicine, and extra equipment were placed in watertight containers, then buried at what Warren felt would be appropriate intervals along the way. These burial sites were marked with small rock cairns, then noted on United States Geological Survey topographic quads.

The canoe departed from Wahweap Marina on Lake Powell's southwest end. An average of 15 to 20 miles was paddled each day of the journey, an effort resulting in muscles so sore that at first Warren could barely move his upper body. It took two weeks before the pace became comfortable and the journey filled with the peaceful contemplation of some of the most beautiful terrain on earth.

This book is the photographic record of that trip, an adventure which included, at one point, the destruction of Warren's camp by a violent winter blizzard. Despite such personal and financial hardships, Warren and his companion, Ely, managed to explore more than 1,000 miles of the magnificent terrain of Lake Powell.

Right: Homba Goshli sailing into Hite Marina—northern end of Lake Powell

Opposite page: Warren and Ely digging up a food drop in Moki Canyon

4

Cliffs of the Rainbow Plateau as seen from Cornerstone Canyon

Magnificent cliffs reflected on the calm surface

6

Glen Canyon Dam and Bridge on the Colorado River

Glen Canyon Dam and Bridge

Glen Canyon Dam, located on the Arizona-Utah border, rises 710 feet from a bedrock foundation. A concrete and steel base, 340 feet wide, spans the 1,500 feet that separate the walls of the canyon. The thick support is in sharp contrast to the crest of the structure, which is only 25 feet wide.

The first bucket of concrete was poured on June 17, 1960, and the pouring continued twenty-four hours a day, seven days a week, until September 13, 1963. The dam and adjoining power plant required 5,105,000 cubic yards of concrete in all.

The power plant was designed for eight generators, creating 900,000 kilowatts of hydroelectric power. However, the popularity of the region and the growth of communities using this power source have resulted in moves to increase the plant's productivity.

The steel arch bridge is the highest and the second longest of its kind in the United States. The arch is 1,028 feet in length and supports a bridge deck of 1,271 feet, suspended 700 feet above the Colorado River. The bridge was built in two parts, each starting from an opposite side of the river. The crews miscalculated their connecting point by less than three quarters of an inch. They corrected the problem by pushing the two parts together by hand, then riveting them into place.

Just viewing the results of this seemingly impossible project is a breathtaking experience. Yet the more you know about the history of the land, both before and after it was altered to form Lake Powell, the better you will be able to enjoy your visit. You may wish to utilize the visitors' center on the canyon's edge, overlooking the lake and surrounding area. There are displays, books, films, and self-guided tours of the dam available at the center that will help you better understand and appreciate the awesome splendor, a unique creation of God and man.

Velvet Waters

The Colorado River once raged through mountain wilderness, its turbulence so intense that the land was transformed into a mélange of mesas, buttes, arches, coves, and cliffs. Then, with the construction of the dam, the ravaging onslaught of water was transformed into the gently flowing Lake Powell, a deep, blue mirror, its tranquil surface reflecting the constantly changing panorama of clouds, sky, sun, and moon.

All around Lake Powell are high cliffs and red desert sands, yet the melting mountain snow maintains the cool waters, so perfect for year-around recreation. No other desert in the world has so much water flowing across its surface as does this area of the American Southwest.

Almost every size of craft can be enjoyed on these velvet waters, from small canoes to houseboats on which you can spend days or weeks exploring the terrain. Yet even the most experienced boater must keep in mind that there can be problems caused by the variety of craft using the lake, as well as by natural phenomena affecting the water.

Whenever the lake narrows, precautions must be taken when larger boats are around. These can leave three- to five-foot waves in their wake, waves high enough to endanger smaller craft. Other waves are formed naturally, through the slow erosion of sandstone cliffs. Small portions of the cliff occasionally break loose, plummeting into the lake. The shock waves move across the channels, then rebound with slightly less force, until gradually the waters are again serene.

8

Right: Calm waters on Padre Bay

10

Evening reflection in Padre Bay

Dark blue storm waters in Five Mile Stretch

11

Canyon Walls

No matter where you travel along Lake Powell, the ever-changing views might be likened to an open-air museum of natural history. Your first sights are often the overpowering cliffs whose subtle shadings of color, texture, light, and shadow, so prominent in early morning and late afternoon, make the paintings of the great masters seem as child's play.

For centuries, the rocks have experienced the slow erosion of rain that has gently streaked the surface of the walls, creating a patina the color of oxidizing copper. The softer sandstone cliffs have deep gorges cut in all directions along their surfaces.

There are the monuments to nature's past fury. Round a bend in the lake and suddenly you are faced with the high, cone-shaped mound of Navajo Mountain, a long-inactive volcano. The terrain is so forbidding that the Hopi Indians speak of a legend told by the "old people" which forbids travel or dwelling in what they called the "great water chasm." Yet other tribes did visit there, and arrowheads may still be found, remnants of the Paiutes and Navajos who crossed the land long ago while hunting.

Little change is found in the stratigraphic formations of Lake Powell's surrounding canyon lands as the waters move from western Colorado to southeastern Nevada, and from northern New Mexico to central Utah. The topography remains a magnificent blend of terraced plateaus, cliff-bound mesas, monoclinal ridges, and deep, vertical-walled canyons. No matter where you travel in the region, the beauty of the terrain is a breathtaking experience, unique within the United States.

Above: Sunrise strikes a cliff in Forbidding Canyon

13

Shading and shadows dramatize the landscape

14

15

Above: Face Canyon dead ends into sheer walls   Inset: Leisengang Banding—the chemical precipitation of iron oxide

Opposite page: A tapestry wall reaches skyward near the San Juan River

Majestic cliffs meet calm water

The Vegetation

Vegetation is sparse around Lake Powell. What little soil exists is derived from the rocks and lacks essential minerals for most plant life. The ground water is also insufficient to aid growth, yet visitors are continuously delighted with the rugged beauty of those plants that manage to survive despite all the obstacles to their existence.

The grass, when it grows, is found in bunches, as though the blades have united for mutual protection. The trees are found in small groves near the canyon ends; weeds, often bearing flowers of great beauty, appear unexpectedly amid the rocks.

It is during the spring that Lake Powell's vegetation is most beautiful. The desert cactus bursts into bloom and wildflowers abound along the shoreline and beaches. The vegetation, though limited, enhances the rugged beauty of the rocky terrain.

A barrel cactus blooms, defying the harsh terrain and difficult existence

19

Above: Sego Lily, Utah state flower   Insets: Cactus blossoms

Opposite page: A gnarled tree is mute testimony to a desolate land   Inset: Spring life

Antelope Island

Antelope Island is both one of the oldest and newest of the scenic attractions of Lake Powell. The island, which at this writing has yet to be stocked with antelope, was created in June of 1973 when the water level receded enough to uncover the land. However, long before the dam was built, Antelope Island was the campsite for the Domínguez-Escalante Expedition of 1776.

Francisco Atanasio Domínguez and Silvestre Vélez de Escalante were members of the Spanish Order of Friars Minor—the Franciscans. They volunteered to explore the lands of the new world that existed between New Mexico and California at a time when the British colonists were fighting the Revolutionary War. The Franciscans hoped to open a road system to provide a more effective linking of the various Spanish Catholic missionary outposts. The two friars led a small, unarmed party that succeeded in traveling from what is now known as Santa Fe, New Mexico, through western Colorado, central Utah (where they turned back because of inclement weather), northern Arizona, and western New Mexico. It was a major feat of exploration at the time. For part of the journey, the party stayed on a high ridge directly across from Navajo Canyon.

The island's southwestern corner was the stopping point for Major John Wesley Powell's Colorado River expedition, though the location was then known as Sentinel Rock. The last spur of land, now called Castle Rock, was used for background images during the filming of the motion picture *The Greatest Story Ever Told.*

The creation of Antelope Island and a channel known as Castle Rock Cut-off, running between Castle Rock and Antelope Island, has made boating much safer for travelers on Lake Powell. In the early years of the lake, all boats traveled through the high-walled channel of Glen Canyon. This was an area known as the Narrows and it was not large enough to safely support the volume of traffic. The new channel not only provides a far better alternative route, it also saves twenty miles when sailing up the lake.

Antelope Island is an excellent stopping point when traveling Lake Powell. It is located directly opposite Wahweap Marina, and its highest point is 230 feet above the

lake. The view is spectacular, and the fact that the island is only 30 miles in circumference means that you can enjoy a weekend hike, camping halfway around the island one night and completing the trek the next day.

On the island's southeast corner is an area which was a quarry site for various Indian tribes. They used the river cobble, stones washed in by the water, to make their tools and weapons.

The ridgeline itself is interesting because of its intricacies. Many large alcoves have been cut by water running through small ravines and gullies; the result is natural coloring of impressive beauty.

There are excellent campsites along Antelope Island, and the wildlife which still exists is a fascinating mix. There are coyotes, foxes, packrats, ringtail cats, seagulls, ravens, hawks, migratory ducks, geese, eagles, and an occasional swan. Cattle, which once grazed the land, have been removed.

Above: Ancient layered sand dunes on Antelope Island

Above: A storm ends on the island

Opposite page: Wind-sculptured sandstone

23

24

Spectacular sunset over Lone Rock as seen from Antelope Island

The Hazards

Before continuing with the beauties of Lake Powell, it is important to note that some precautions must be taken. Lake Powell is a relatively narrow lake surrounded by canyons which can cause wind storms to become unexpectedly violent forces.

A storm begins rapidly, with wind racing through the canyons and churning the lake's surface into an uncontrollable frenzy. The sky will grow dark, the velvet mirror lake reflecting the gray, then black fury of the storm.

Funnels, much like tornadoes, will dip to the ground, spreading debris and whipping sand into what feels like millions of tiny darts if you are caught in its path. At other times, wind currents traveling from separate directions will be drawn together in a violent collision. Huge waves, lacking direction, will thrash about the lake, endangering those who failed to return to land when the storm was first sighted. Large tour boats have been known to be tossed as easily as wood chips during these moments of watery violence.

Fortunately, storms pass quickly on Lake Powell. It is unusual for one to stay more than thirty minutes before moving on and restoring the natural calm of the area.

The rushing torrent of the Colorado River once carried driftwood in its wake. The wood fell from trees in the high mountains of Colorado and Utah, traveling like miniature water craft along the downhill run of the river. However, with the construction of the dam, the driftwood was stopped in its flow, then deposited in Lake Powell where it can be a hazard for both boaters and water skiers. Even a small piece can puncture the hull of a rapidly moving boat, bend a prop, or be tossed against a water skier with such force that legs can be shattered.

Ely and I experienced this problem first-hand when, during a storm, our canoe was pitched onto a large log. The choppy wave jammed that log between the boat's pontoons and hull. All control was lost until the wind subsided and I could finally reach shore to make necessary repairs—a half day later.

The formation of Lake Powell by flooding forced by the construction of Glen Canyon Dam created small islands from what were once high land masses. The sandstone

and slickrock provide limited footing for climbing, and often the eroding cliffs cause rims to crumble without warning. The islands have few hazards for the careful day visitor. There are, however, scorpions that come out during the night. Overnight campers should be aware of these poisonous insects.

The greatest danger faced on Lake Powell seems the least harmful: the sun. As Arizona-Utah skies lack many of the pollutants and cloud covers found in other parts of the United States, the radiation is intense. The reflection of the sun on the water adds to its intensity. Severe sunburning is possible on the beach or on your boat. Wear a hat or other protective head covering, and use any tanning lotion containing a sun screen. No matter what other precautions you take, wear clothing that will protect you from the direct rays of the sun. On the water it is possible to begin to sunburn within ten minutes. Protective measures will keep your trip an enjoyable one.

Educate yourself in desert dangers and survival before spending much time on Lake Powell or within Glen Canyon National Recreation Area. Otherwise, the area's beauty and tranquility may prevent you from being wary of the dangers of the environment and of the occasionally harsh climate.

Above: Storm brewing on the lake

Opposite page: Homba Goshli in tow

28

Storm stirs up rough water

Glen Canyon's Colorful History

The rich history of the Glen Canyon area would fill many books. There are stories of explorers and Indians, of violence, hardships forced by nature, and great heroism in the midst of adversity. Yet when you look at the map of the area, there are two sites which are likely to arouse your curiosity because of their unusual names. These are known as Harvey's Fear and Teddy's Horse Pasture.

The naming of Harvey's Fear dates back to the early 1900s, a time when Mormon ranchers drove their stock from Escalante, Hurricane, and Cannonville out onto Kaiparowits Plateau. There, the cows and horses would be allowed to graze amidst lush green grass and numerous springs and water holes.

The ranchers were successful, and gradually brought more and more livestock to forage. This increase meant that more land was needed, and eventually, the range was depleted. The animals grazed to the very edge of Kaiparowits Plateau, where a sheer cliff wall drops 800 feet.

The cliff walls were almost impossible for man or animals to scale, yet when the ranchers looked down, they saw even more verdant grazing land. It was not long before a ranch hand named Harvey Watts finally devised a way to build a trail from Kaiparowits down into the Dry Rock Creek Canyon, where so many acres of grass and water awaited the animals.

As the story goes, the area was named for Watts's hair-raising experience. Harvey, on horseback, was ram-rodding steers down the trail when the lead steer balked and refused to go any further. Harvey dismounted and carefully edged his way through the tightly grouped animals in an effort to reach the recalcitrant leader. He moved slowly and steadily, as one false step could send him careening over the cliff. Unfortunately, Harvey's caution was to no avail: with a toss of his horns, a steer knocked him over the side.

The cliff was steep, but Harvey was lucky. Able to grab the exposed roots of a cliffside bush, he hung for hours, clinging to the shrub that supported his weight but did not allow him to climb back onto the trail. Finally, he was found and pulled back up, onto solid ground.

Harvey and his friends never forgot this experience, and they immortalized it by naming this section of the Kaiparowits Plateau and the trail into the canyon, "Harvey's Fear."

Teddy's Horse Pasture was named for Edward "Teddy" Wilcox, a Mormon ranch hand who developed a trail into Cornerstone and Dangling Rope canyons. The trail wound across the sand hills below Billy Flat Top, around the ledges of Glen Canyon, and provided the means for thousands of horses to reach a pasture which ultimately

Above: Natural sentinel as seen from Dry Rock Creek Canyon

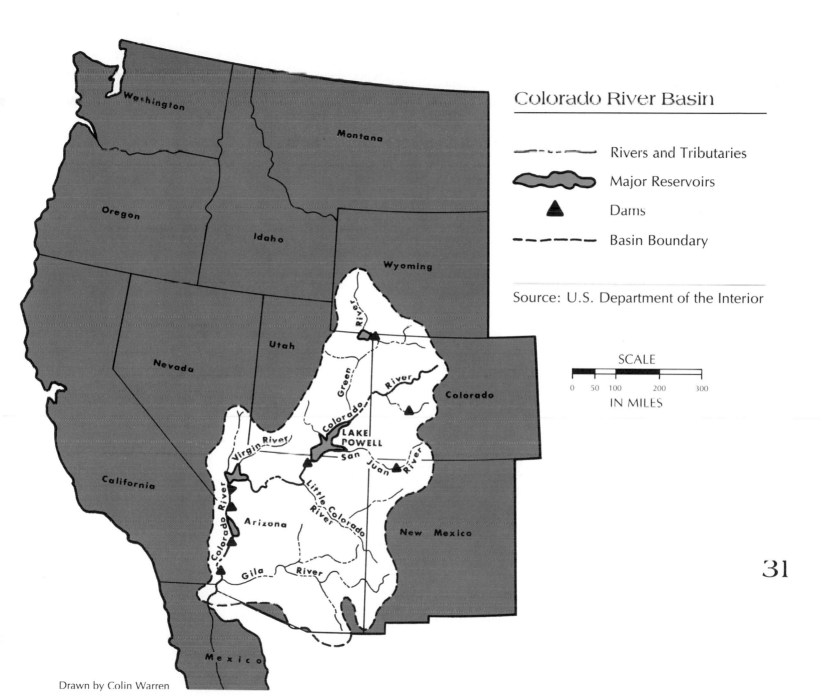

Colorado River Basin

— · — · — Rivers and Tributaries

Major Reservoirs

▲ Dams

– – – – Basin Boundary

Source: U.S. Department of the Interior

SCALE

0   50 100   200   300
IN MILES

Washington

Montana

Oregon

Idaho

Wyoming

Utah

Nevada

Colorado

California

Arizona

New Mexico

Green River

Colorado River

LAKE POWELL

San Juan River

Virgin River

Little Colorado River

Colorado River

Gila River

Mexico

31

Drawn by Colin Warren

covered 25,000 acres. With grazing, the passage of time, and the creation of Lake Powell, most of the land was lost and the existing grass is no longer good. However, in homage to bygone days, the area remains known as Teddy's Horse Pasture.

Today it is easiest to spot Teddy's Horse Pasture by looking for the remains of a rock fence and log gate used to keep the horses from returning home on their own initiative. Just below Cornerstone Canyon, Teddy's trail narrows and there the fence was erected, the remains of which can still be viewed. The range grasses are almost gone, but magnificent wildflowers and cactus blossoms carpet the land every spring.

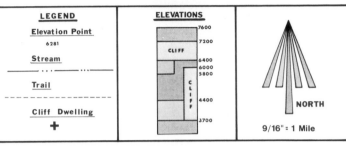

MAP OF
HARVEY'S FEAR
&
TEDDY'S HORSE PASTURE
Lake Powell, Glen Canyon National Recreation Area, Utah

LEGEND

Elevation Point
6281

Stream

Trail

Cliff Dwelling
+

ELEVATIONS

7600
7200
CLIFF
6400
6000
5800
CLIFF
4400
3700

NORTH

9/16" = 1 Mile

NUMERICAL INDEX

1 Rock fence & log gate

2 Dangling Rope Canyon

3 Dangling Rope Marina

4 Standing Rock

5 Cornerstone Canyon

6 Balanced Rock Canyon

7 Klondike Cove

8 Driftwood Canyon

9 East End Spring

10 Maple Seeps

11 Ernie Moyes/Monk Moyes Spring

12 Cave Spring

13 Twitchell Canyon

14 Friendship Cove

15 Dungeon Canyon

16 Grotto Canyon

17 Wetherill Canyon

18 Mountain Sheep Canyon

19 Little Arch Canyon

20 Cathedral Canyon

AREA MAP

Hite
Lake Powell
Wahweap

Drawn by: Colin A. Warren

Date: April 22, 1983

SOURCE

1. Landsat satellite photo image

2. U.S. Geological Survey

3. U.S. Park Service

4. Field research & survey

NOTES

1. This map is intended to show general geographic outlines & should not be used for hiking or navigation.

2. Elevations shown are in feet above mean sea level.

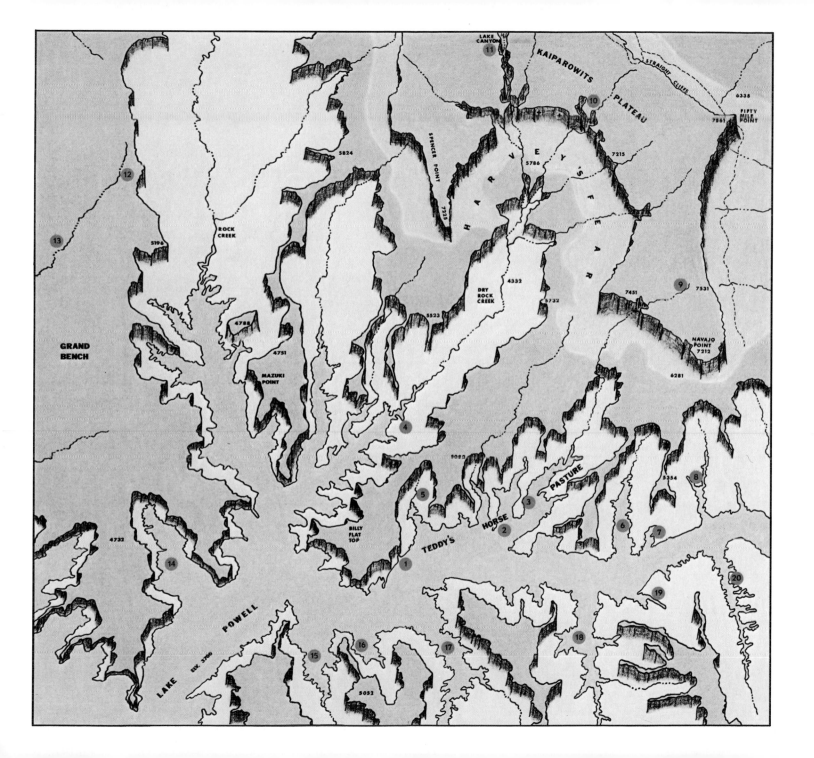

Boundary Butte

The novelty of crossing from one state to another by virtue of a simple paddle stroke or footstep is one of the curiosities of Lake Powell. The Arizona-Utah border, for example, is marked by a slab of sandstone with "Arizona" chiseled into one side and "Utah" into the other. The vintage 1910 slab, one of the few boundary markers still standing, is situated along latitude 37° 00′ N, which is also the location of what has come to be called Boundary Butte.

Flanked by Padre Point and Labyrinth and Face canyons, Boundary Butte was the landmark used by the 1776 Domínguez-Escalante expedition to locate the east crossing point of the then-untamed Colorado River. In the expedition's diary, the ruggedness of the terrain was noted: ". . . the river flows through a very deep gorge [and] everything . . . adjacent to the ford consists of very tall cliffs and precipices."

The modern state boundary line between Arizona and Utah falls across the butte, but the drama of the topography remains much as it was in the days of the Spanish explorers.

Boundary Butte in Labyrinth Canyon

Rainbow Bridge National Monument

Poets speak of a special rainbow, touched by the hand of God and turned to stone. The Navajo Indians agree, having long recognized rainbows as an important element in religious ceremonies meant to insure adequate rain for survival. Geologists talk of erosion, the slow wearing away of mountains and the natural shifting of terrain, as the creative force behind the graceful arching symmetry so magnificent to behold. Whoever may be correct, the reality is that Rainbow Bridge is one of the largest and most awesome of all natural bridges.

Rainbow Bridge rises 290 feet above the creek bed and spans 275 feet with a center width of 33 feet, adequate to support two lanes of automobile traffic. The surface is extremely smooth and treacherous, and the curvature is so great that crossing it can be very dangerous. As a result, the Park Service has limited access to the bridge.

One side of the arch, carved from a single massive block of cross-bedded Navajo sandstone, rises from a base encircled by the ancient waters of Bridge Creek. The other section of this natural bridge is firmly buttressed against the canyon wall. This positioning has provided scientists with a possible geological explanation for its creation.

Rainbow Bridge probably began 200 million years ago when there was a wet era in what is known as the Triassic Period. Vast quantities of sediment came together to form the base of the bridge. Then, as arid periods followed, windblown dust was deposited in the form of mammoth dunes. Eventually, periods of tropical climatic conditions and the slow evolution, then disappearance, of deep ancient seas led to the hardening of the dunes into what is now known as Navajo sandstone.

Perhaps 60 million years ago, there was extreme tectonic activity, causing major shifts in the land. Navajo Mountain rose to a height of over 10,000 feet. Water poured down the mountain slopes, slowly eroding the land and creating Bridge Creek, Bridge Canyon, and finally Rainbow Bridge. This solid spur of sandstone extending from the canyon wall impeded the passage of the creek. The waters constantly raced against the lower section, eventually creating the window which gives this natural bridge the appearance of a rainbow. Then, with the passage of still more time, the course of the

Rainbow Bridge

37

water shifted from the ancient meander on the east side of the bridge and today follows the shorter, steeper course of travel under the spur.

Gradually, Rainbow Bridge was scaled and undermined, narrowing the width, then increasing the height and length. The beauty and unusual appearance so impressed the Indians who viewed it that it became an object of both worship and fear. It was little known to Anglo explorers until August 14, 1909, when Dr. Byron Cummings, dean of the University of Utah, and a party of adventurers were led by Nasja-Begay, a Paiute shepherd, to what was called the "Rainbow Turned to Stone."

President William H. Taft and members of Congress were so fascinated by the discovery that Rainbow Bridge National Monument was created soon after. The formal proclamation was signed on May 30, 1910, setting aside 150 acres for the monument.

The creation of Lake Powell has made Rainbow Bridge National Monument readily accessible for the first time, though the flooding from Glen Canyon Dam destroyed many of the surrounding rock structures the Navajo consider to have important religious significance. Many of the visitors feel as author Zane Grey did when, in his book *Rainbow Trail,* he spoke of an encounter with the bridge, stating in part:

"A mile beyond, all was bright with the colors of sunset, and spanning the cañon in the graceful shape and beautiful hues of a rainbow was a magnificent stone bridge . . . this thing was glorious. It silenced him, yet did not stun or awe. His body and brain, weary and dull from the toils of travel, received a singular and revivifying freshness . . . A rainbow magnified . . . no longer transparent and ethereal, but solidified, a thing of ages sweeping up majestically from the red walls, its iris-hued arch against the blue sky.

"Ages before life had evolved upon the earth, it had spread its grand arch from wall to wall, black and mystic at night, transparent and rose in the sunrise, at sunset, a flaming curve limned against the heavens. When the race of man has passed, it would, perhaps, stand there still . . ."

Opposite page: The symmetry of reflection—Navajo Mountain, Rainbow Bridge

Awe-inspiring heights of Rainbow Bridge

Navajo Mountain

The Navajo Indian Reservation borders Lake Powell's southwest shore, from Glen Canyon Dam to the San Juan River on the north side of the volcanic creation now known as Navajo Mountain. For the Indians, the volcanic dome, whose shape is in striking contrast with the harsh mountains all around, is *Naatsis'aan,* or "Head of Earth Woman." It was originally a place of bad spirits, a land mass to be avoided, though the reasons for this fear are no longer known.

The mountain is actually what is known as a laccolith. Its volcanic core pushed up some 60 million years ago, carrying the surrounding land with it. The central core never broke through the earth's surface, a fact known because there is no igneous rock surrounding the mountain as there would be with such a break. Whether stories of this volcanic movement were part of Navajo history, or if there was some other reason for the fear, is uncertain. It was not until 1863 that the Navajos first accepted the mountain as a haven.

During the Civil War, Navajos, led by Nashkeniinii, came upon the mountain while fleeing the U.S. Cavalry. They entered the north side of the mountain, an area that the cavalry was unable to penetrate. The Navajos were saved and, as is the practice with their religious beliefs, they determined that special gods, not luck, were responsible for their safety.

Naatsis'aan gave birth to Monster Slayer and, together, the two gods placed themselves as shields to protect Nashkeniinii's band from the army. Thus special religious ceremonies related to the protection of the people are held on the mountain, as well as rites relating to rain.

Again according to Navajo legend, there is a holy spring atop Head of Earth Woman (Navajo Mountain) from which young clouds are born. These clouds darken, moving out as thunderous rainstorms. Because of the air currents in the area, clouds gathering over Navajo Mountain usually foretell the occasional violent storms which bring torrential rain to neighboring Page and Wahweap.

Navajo Mountain has a tree-laden slope and a relatively flat surface of over 200 acres. Erosion of the sides has exposed brilliantly colored sandstone. Much of Lake Powell can be seen by hiking around the base of the mountain; visitors often go higher.

Navajo Mountain's crest exhibits the weathering effects of frost wedging, and the work of ice is shown by the large, angular blocks of rock that extend down the mountain as rock streams. The north and west faces of the mountain have been vigorously eroded, with deep canyons cut by water run-off; streams fall at 800 feet to the mile. The canyons are separated by high, thin ridges which extend up the mountain's flanks.

When exploring here, remember that the mountain is sacred Navajo land and part of the Navajo reservation. Be certain to obtain permission from the Navajo Tribal Government before venturing onto the mountain itself.

Above: Clouds gather over Navajo Mountain

Opposite page: Ethereal view of Navajo Mountain

44

Man-Made Attractions

There are two points of interest often mentioned in conjunction with Lake Powell, both of which were created by man. One, Rainbow Marina, served boaters in the area for fifteen years before being dismantled in 1982. The other, commonly known as "Franker's Tanker," continues to ply the waters.

Rainbow Marina was located at Rainbow Harbor near the area called Forbidding Canyon. There was a harbor, a gas dock, and delightful aromas from Papa Lloyd Mennard's crappie chowder and Walapai Johnny's beans and biscuits. Houseboats often anchored for days or weeks, and fish such as striped bass, shad, and crappie abounded.

Rainbow Marina was unique in that it was a self-contained community. It generated its own electricity, purified its own water, treated its sewage and maintained floating fuel tanks to serve the boaters. It could only be reached by water.

The rainstorms brought a special beauty to the area, a beauty which can still be witnessed although the marina is now dismantled. Waterfalls were instant creations of the storms, beginning with a slow trickle, then changing to a thunderous roar as thousands of gallons fell hundreds of feet from the high cliffs to the lake below.

Less spectacular but still of interest is the tanker ship called "Chevron Service." It was built in Astoria, Oregon, in 1954, and for the next fifteen years was used to haul fuel from Seattle, Washington, to Alaska. Then the ship, which is fifty-two feet long

Above: Rainbow Marina in Forbidding Canyon
Opposite page: A view of snow-capped Navajo Mountain from Cascade Canyon

and holds ten thousand gallons of gasoline, was severed and brought to Lake Powell, where it was welded back together.

The pilot of "Chevron Service" for many years was a man named Frank Smith whose love for the craft and friendliness toward the people he served on Lake Powell resulted in the vessel being called "Franker's Tanker." Typically, it is loaded with fuel, from one hundred to two hundred cases of beer and soda, blocks of ice in the cargo hold, and has as many as three garbage barges in tow. An aquatic train, weaving its way at a snail's pace among the mesas and buttes of the lake, Franker's Tanker is a floating service station in a vast and watery terrain.

Above: Even Franker's Tanker seems insignificant next to the towering cliffs

Opposite page: Franker's Tanker on patrol

*From Rainbow Marina dock . . . a quiet
moment reflected*

Sunrise lights the cliffs at Rainbow Marina

49

50

Photographing Lake Powell

The greatest beauty of Lake Powell is captured in the early morning and the late afternoon. Dawn strikes the lake and the surrounding mountains with a rainbow of colors. First there is purple, exaggerating the green of the foliage and trees along Navajo Mountain. Then slowly the sky begins to warm, and red, orange, and yellow dominate the light.

The lower angles of morning and late afternoon sunlight cross the face of the mountains, revealing their texture and constantly changing colors. Golden sun reflects against the lake, backlighting some of the mountains and spotlighting others. Often you can record breathtaking scenes by focusing on the reflections of the water.

Photographing the setting sun requires large quantities of film. As you watch the lake and the surrounding terrain, each small descent of the sun on the horizon seems to create an entirely new color scheme. Subtle shadings of the earth are revealed for a few moments, then retreat as other images take their place. The land never changes, standing as it has for centuries, but the appearance seems a kaleidoscope delightful to record.

Any camera will produce good photographs of Lake Powell; those settings that are meant for the brightest sun are most often used if your camera is adjustable. The light is strong, so slow-speed color films are recommended. I used Kodachrome for much of this book, even toward sunset when the light was fading rapidly. Color print film is also effective, though, again, the slower films are best.

If you have a fixed-lens camera, photographing from a boat will allow the greatest flexibility. You will be able to move closer to objects in the distance, filling your frame in ways which will not be so easy from land.

51

Opposite page: Waterfall in Rainbow Harbor

Photo Tips

Look at the natural rock formations for framing ideas. You can often frame a scene through the spaces in the rocks, much as I did when recording Rainbow Bridge. Trees and shrubs also make good framing devices.

When photographing wildflowers, try to get as close as possible. If you have a fixed-lens camera, an interesting effect can be obtained by placing your camera low to the ground and shooting across the carpet of flowers. This compensates for your inability to move in close on a single plant.

If you have an adjustable camera and are using slide film, you can *saturate your colors* by exposing one-half F-stop less than your meter recommends.

No matter what type of camera you are using, *try to keep the light meter from pointing directly at the sun.* The harsh light can temporarily blind your meter, causing the next few pictures to be incorrectly exposed.

Protect your camera from water. Some photographers use plastic sandwich bags to hold cameras and lenses when not in use, even though they may be kept in a gadget bag.

Take plenty of film. You will be in a boat, with far more picture-taking opportunities than you might normally experience. Carry extra batteries, even if the batteries in your camera are fresh. You can store both film and batteries in a picnic cooler or even a wide-mouth insulated container, such as a thermos, to protect them from the hot sun.

The sun can damage camera and film. Left in a hot car while parking to arrange for your boat or even when near the windows of a houseboat, *your gear must be protected.* On the water, keep the lens pointed away from the sunlight, except when taking pictures. It is best to keep a lens cap or other covering on the lens, which can act like a magnifying glass, burning a hole in your shutter. The sun's heat can also alter the chemistry of your film so that colors will not be exact. Keeping the camera in a picnic cooler, wrapped in plastic if ice or liquid is inside, will help protect it when you are not taking photographs.

If you are taking a new camera along on your visit, *experiment with it before you leave home.* You want to be certain you have no problems when you reach the magnificent scenery of Lake Powell and Glen Canyon.

53

Sunrise over Good Hope Bay

54

Car headlights dwarfed by the spectacular sunset

The setting sun ignites the cliff in Padre Bay

A cave near the San Juan River frames Glen Canyon

Dangling Rope Canyon

57

Light variations

58

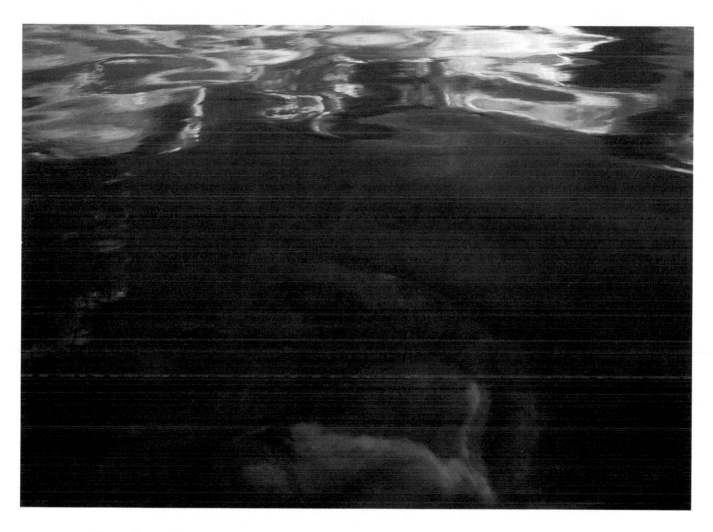

59

The surface of the water creates an unusual effect

60

CONCLUSION

I hope the pictures in this book have whetted your appetite for your own visit to Lake Powell and the Glen Canyon National Recreation Area. When I first decided to take Ely on a year-long adventure on the water, the reaction to my proposed trip was varied. Those who knew the area understood. The constantly changing scenery, the overwhelming majesty of the mountains, the velvet blue waters serenely flowing past dwellings used by ancient Indians, steep waterfalls, towering cliffs, and all the other attractions of the area have an appeal as overwhelming as the Siren songs of ancient mythology. Those who had never visited the region were surprised by the appeal; nowhere else in the United States can such varied grandeur be found, and they could not imagine the area's attraction.

There were storms at times, and my canoe was ravaged by their violence. Ely and I had to be rescued from a blizzard. There were nights we huddled together for warmth. Yet our journey was a culmination of two loves: mine for the natural beauty that is Lake Powell, and the companionship of man and dog, a symbiotic relationship that was to be the final lengthy journey we shared.

Now I have left Glen Canyon, and Ely is no longer with me. In the way of older dogs who are blissfully unaware of the passage of time, he died of a heart attack while chasing a female for whom he had taken a fancy. The travails and joys of our Lake Powell trip were our last experiences together.

On my next trip to Powell, I will probably be alone. I had thought that, after years of working in the area during the off-seasons, this trip recording the seemingly endless wonders would be my last. As you will see when you visit the area, however, the haunting beauty keeps you returning again and again, to thrill anew at the everchanging panorama of one of our most magnificent national treasures.

Opposite page: Fading light and late sunset colors provide a dramatic backdrop

Facts and Figures

LAKE POWELL

Length: 186 miles   **Capacity:** 28,000,000 acre feet   **Surface Area:** 162,700 acres   **Shoreline Length:** Averages 1,900 linear miles depending on surface elevation

   Photo Tip: Slower-speed color and black-and-white films are best. If your camera is adjustable, settings will usually be for the brightest sunlight. To avoid underexposure, point your meter towards rocks and away from the water when taking a light reading.

GLEN CANYON DAM

Height: 710 feet from base to crest, 580 feet above river bed   **Crest Length:** 1,500 feet   **Crest Width:** 25 feet   **Base Width:** 340 feet   **Concrete:** 5,105,000 cubic yards

   Photo Tip: A wide-angle lens is helpful to capture the splendor. Try to keep the camera so that the film plane is parallel with the perpendicular sides of the dam to avoid distortion.

GLEN CANYON BRIDGE

Height above river: 700 feet   **Arch:** 1,028 feet   **Deck Length:** 1,271 feet

   Photo Tip: Experiment with angles and lenses. Wide-angle photos across the span may not be as interesting as isolating segments, such as with a moderate (135mm lens on 35mm camera) telephoto. Try exposing for bright sun, then taking the picture in early morning or late afternoon when you can silhouette parts of the span.

COLORADO RIVER

Length: 1,440 miles from Rocky Mountains to Gulf of Mexico   **Drainage Area:** 243,000 square miles   **Average Rainfall:** Varies from five inches a year in the southern deserts to fifty inches in the Rocky Mountains

   Photo Tip: Take advantage of morning and afternoon reflections for interesting mirror effects of mountains near the water. Reflections also have an appeal during sunset and as storm clouds gather. Focus on the image of the subject being reflected, not the surface of the water itself, to be certain your picture will be sharp.

RAINBOW BRIDGE

Height: 290 feet above the creek bed   **Span:** 275 feet   **Width at top:** 33 feet

   Photo Tip: Try using Rainbow Bridge as a framing device. With a wide-angle lens, focus through the bridge, letting the silhouetted shape enhance your picture. Take the light-meter reading from the subject to be recorded, not from the bridge itself.

Serene reflections in Oak Canyon

63

64

Above: Vast views intensified by early-morning shadows

Opposite page: The sun's final glory ends another adventure on the velvet waters

BIBLIOGRAPHY

Ambler, Richard J. *The Anasazi.* Flagstaff: Museum of Northern Arizona, 1977.

Briggs, Walter. *Without Noise of Arms: The 1776 Domínguez-Escalante Search for a Route from Santa Fe to Monterey.* Flagstaff, Arizona: Northland Press, 1976.

Canby, Thomas Y. "The Anasazi: Riddles in the Ruins." *National Geographic* 162, no. 5 (November, 1982): 562–92.

Crump, Donald J., ed. *The Desert Realm.* Washington, D.C.: Special Publications Division, National Geographic Society, 1982.

Edwards, Walter Meayers. "Lake Powell: Waterway to Desert Wonders." *National Geographic* 132, no. 1 (July, 1967): 44–75.

Findley, Rowe. "Miracle of the Potholes." *National Geographic* 148, no. 4 (October, 1975): 570–79.

Glen Canyon Dam. Washington, D.C.: U.S. Government Printing Office, OF-574577, 1960.

Gregory, Herbert E. "Geology of the Navajo Country," Professional Paper No. 93. Washington, D.C.: U.S. Government Printing Office, 1917.

Gregory, Herbert E. and Raymond C. Moore. "The Kaiparowits Region," Professional Paper No. 164. Washington, D.C.: U.S. Government Printing Office, 1931.

Grey, Zane. *The Rainbow Trail.* England: Ian Henry Publication, 1982.

Luckert, Karl W. *Navajo Mountain and Rainbow Bridge Religion.* Flagstaff: Museum of Northern Arizona, 1977.

McKee, Edwin D. *Ancient Landscapes of the Grand Canyon Region.* Flagstaff, Arizona: Northland Press, 1982.

Miller, David E., ed. *The Route of Domínguez-Escalante Expedition, 1776–77.* Salt Lake City: Utah State Historical Society, 1976.

Powell, J. W. *The Exploration of the Colorado River and Its Canyons.* Washington, D.C.: Smithsonian Institute, 1895. Reprint. New York: Dover Press, 1961.

Rabbitt, Mary C. *John Wesley Powell's Exploration of the Colorado River.* Washington, D.C.: U.S. Government Printing Office, 0-261-226/10, 1978.

———. *John Wesley Powell, Soldier-Explorer-Scientist.* Washington, D.C.: U.S. Government Printing Office, 311-348/44, 1980.